About Author

Kamlesh Vishwakarma is a seasoned professional in the field of online marketing, renowned for his extensive 24 years of experience and expertise in technology and social media. As an Amazon-verified Advertising Partner, he showcases his credibility and proficiency in online advertising. Kamlesh consistently demonstrates strategic thinking abilities, adeptly crafting compelling content, managing advertising campaigns, and fostering online communities. His adeptness in harnessing the power of Amazon ads translates into tangible and impactful results.

Understanding Quick Commerce

The Rise of Quick Commerce: A Retail Revolution

In the fast-paced world of modern retail, consumer expectations are evolving rapidly. Traditional e-commerce, which once seemed revolutionary with its two-day delivery promises, is now being outpaced by the next big shift: **quick commerce (q-commerce)**. This new model prioritizes ultra-fast delivery, often within 10 to 30 minutes, reshaping the way consumers shop and businesses operate.

What is Quick Commerce?

Quick commerce refers to the rapid delivery of groceries, household essentials, and other small consumer goods through hyper-local fulfillment networks. Unlike traditional e-commerce, which relies on large warehouses, q-commerce depends on micro-fulfillment centers or dark stores located in urban areas, ensuring swift last-mile delivery.

Why is Quick Commerce Booming?

Several factors contribute to the rise of q-commerce:

- **Changing Consumer Behavior** – Convenience-driven shoppers increasingly demand instant gratification. The rise of food delivery apps has conditioned consumers to expect products almost immediately.
- **Urbanization & Population Density** – High-density cities provide the perfect setting for quick commerce, making last-mile logistics efficient.

- **Technology & AI** – Advanced AI-powered logistics, predictive inventory management, and automated warehouses make ultra-fast delivery feasible.
- **Investment Surge** – Startups and established retailers alike are pouring billions into q-commerce infrastructure, betting on its long-term profitability.

Challenges & Roadblocks

Despite its rapid growth, quick commerce faces hurdles:

- **Profitability Concerns** – The cost of ultra-fast delivery and maintaining inventory in multiple small warehouses can strain margins.
- **Workforce & Gig Economy Issues** – Delivery riders often face tight schedules and demanding working conditions.
- **Sustainability Questions** – Increased packaging waste and carbon emissions from rapid deliveries pose environmental concerns.

The Future of Quick Commerce

With major players like Getir, Gopuff, and Instacart investing heavily, quick commerce is not just a trend but a long-term industry shift. The future may see:

- **Autonomous deliveries** using drones and robots.
- **Personalized, AI-driven inventory** to reduce wastage and improve efficiency.
- **Sustainability initiatives** to address environmental impacts.

As consumer expectations evolve, businesses that adapt to the quick commerce revolution will gain a competitive edge. While challenges remain, the potential for growth is undeniable.

What Sets Quick Commerce Apart?

Quick commerce (q-commerce) is not just a faster version of traditional e-commerce—it's a fundamental shift in how retail operates. Here's what makes it unique:

1. Speed & Delivery Time - The most defining feature of q-commerce is its ultra-fast delivery, often within 10 to 30 minutes. Traditional e-commerce operates on a same-day or next-day delivery model, while q-commerce aims for instant gratification, catering to consumers' need for speed.

2. Micro-Fulfillment Centers & Dark Stores - Unlike traditional e-commerce, which relies on large warehouses that serve vast regions, q-commerce operates micro-fulfillment centers or dark stores in urban hubs. These are strategically placed in high-demand areas to reduce last-mile delivery times.

3. Limited Product Selection - Q-commerce focuses on high-demand, everyday essentials—groceries, snacks, personal care items, and household products—rather than the vast product ranges of traditional e-commerce giants like Amazon. This curated approach allows for faster picking, packing, and dispatching.

4. AI-Driven Operations & Predictive Demand - Q-commerce platforms use AI and data analytics to anticipate consumer demand, ensuring that local fulfillment centers stock the most in-demand items. This minimizes stockouts and optimizes inventory turnover, making operations more efficient.

5. Gig Economy & On-Demand Workforce - Q-commerce relies heavily on gig workers and fleet-based delivery models, similar to food delivery services. Couriers are assigned deliveries dynamically, ensuring that orders are fulfilled within minutes of being placed.

6. Hyperlocal Business Model - Since q-commerce operates within a small geographical radius, it caters to localized demand patterns. This allows companies to tailor product offerings based on the specific needs of a neighborhood or city.

7. Impulse-Driven & Last-Minute Shopping - Unlike traditional e-commerce, which is often planned, q-commerce caters to spur-of-the-moment purchases—a missing ingredient for dinner, a forgotten household item, or a sudden craving. This demand for instant solutions fuels the q-commerce revolution.

8. Competitive Pricing & Subscription Models - Many q-commerce players offer free or low-cost delivery, bundled with loyalty programs or subscription plans to keep customers engaged. Unlike traditional e-commerce, where bulk purchases may lead to lower prices, q-commerce thrives on small, frequent orders.

Quick commerce isn't just a trend—it's a complete reinvention of retail logistics, driven by speed, technology, and consumer convenience. As urban lifestyles become busier, q-commerce will continue to reshape the way people shop, blending e-commerce with the immediacy of traditional retail.

The Psychology of Instant Gratification

Instant gratification—the desire to receive rewards immediately— has always been a key driver of consumer behavior. In today's digital age, where everything is available at the tap of a screen, quick commerce (q-commerce) is capitalizing on this deeply ingrained psychological tendency. But why are people drawn to ultra-fast delivery, and what makes q-commerce so addictive?

1. The Dopamine Effect: The Joy of Immediate Rewards - When consumers receive what they want instantly, their brains release dopamine, a neurotransmitter linked to pleasure and motivation. This instant reward cycle reinforces behavior, making them more likely to repeat quick purchases in the future.

- Ordering **groceries in 10 minutes** gives immediate satisfaction, eliminating the hassle of shopping.
- Getting **ice cream delivered instantly** on a hot day enhances the pleasure of indulgence.
- Receiving **urgent essentials** like medicine within minutes reduces anxiety and stress.

2. The Need for Convenience: Reducing Friction & Effort - Modern consumers prioritize ease and efficiency. Q-commerce eliminates the friction of traditional shopping—no need to visit a store, browse aisles, or wait in checkout lines. This aligns with the psychological principle of cognitive ease, where people naturally prefer the path of least resistance.

3. The Power of Instant Gratification in Decision-Making - Impulse buying is a key factor in q-commerce success. Unlike traditional e-commerce, where shoppers often compare prices or wait for deals, q-commerce encourages spontaneous purchases due to its instant availability.

- Consumers are less likely to second-guess a purchase when it can be delivered immediately.

- The urgency of "limited-time offers" in q-commerce apps triggers FOMO (fear of missing out).
- AI-driven recommendations personalize suggestions based on previous behaviors, nudging users toward quick, habitual spending.

4. Psychological Ownership: The "It's Already Mine" Effect People tend to feel ownership over something even before they physically possess it. When q-commerce apps show estimated delivery times like "Arriving in 10 minutes", it strengthens the perception that the item already belongs to them, making the waiting period feel shorter and the purchase more satisfying.

5. The Reward Loop: Reinforcing the Habit of Fast Shopping - Every time a consumer successfully gets an item in minutes, it strengthens a habit loop:

1. **Trigger** → A need arises (hunger, missing an item, craving).
2. **Action** → The consumer places a quick order.
3. **Reward** → The product arrives almost instantly, reinforcing the behavior.

Over time, this loop trains consumers to expect instant fulfillment, making traditional shopping feel slow and inconvenient.

The Flip Side: The Downsides of Instant Gratification - While q-commerce satisfies consumer needs quickly, it also raises concerns:

- **Reduced patience** – Consumers may become **less tolerant of delays** in other areas of life.
- **Increased impulsive spending** – The ease of buying small, frequent items can lead to **overspending**.
- **Sustainability concerns** – The demand for rapid delivery increases carbon footprints and packaging waste.

Final Thoughts: The Future of Instant Gratification in Retail

Q-commerce taps into a fundamental human desire: **the need for instant rewards**. As technology advances, businesses will continue to refine ultra-fast fulfillment, making quick commerce even more seamless and psychologically compelling. However, balancing speed with sustainability and responsible consumer habits will be key to its long-term success.

Building a Quick Commerce Business

Key Components of a Quick Commerce Model

A Quick Commerce (Q-Commerce) model relies on speed, efficiency, and convenience to deliver products to customers within minutes or hours. Here are the key components that make it work:

1. Hyperlocal Fulfillment Centers (Dark Stores)

- Small warehouses or micro-fulfillment centers located close to high-demand areas.
- Stock limited but high-demand inventory for rapid dispatch.

2. Technology-Driven Operations

- AI-based inventory management to predict demand and prevent stockouts.
- Route optimization and order batching for faster deliveries.
- Automated order processing and real-time tracking.

3. On-Demand Logistics & Last-Mile Delivery

- Fleet of delivery riders or partnerships with gig workers.
- Use of e-bikes, scooters, or drones for ultra-fast delivery.
- Smart routing and dynamic traffic updates.

4. Mobile-First Customer Experience

- Intuitive apps and websites for quick ordering.
- Seamless payment options including wallets, UPI, and subscriptions.
- Personalized recommendations and AI-powered search.

5. Limited but Essential Inventory

- Focus on high-frequency, fast-moving consumer goods (FMCG).
- Categories like groceries, personal care, medicines, and essentials.
- Dynamic stock replenishment based on demand trends.

6. Data-Driven Decision Making

- Predictive analytics for customer preferences and peak demand times.
- AI-driven pricing strategies and targeted promotions.
- Customer feedback loops for service improvements.

7. Strategic Partnerships

- Collaboration with local brands, suppliers, and cloud kitchens.
- Vendor-managed inventory to reduce overhead costs.
- Third-party logistics (3PL) integration for scalability.

8. Sustainability Measures

- Eco-friendly packaging and delivery methods.
- Carbon footprint reduction through electric vehicles and optimized routes.
- Incentives for sustainable shopping behaviors.

Technology & Infrastructure: The Backbone of Speed

The success of Quick Commerce (Q-Commerce) relies heavily on a robust technological ecosystem and a well-structured infrastructure. These elements work together to ensure ultra-fast deliveries, seamless operations, and a superior customer experience.

1. AI-Powered Inventory Management

- Predictive analytics forecasts demand and prevents stockouts.
- Automated restocking ensures availability of high-demand products.
- Smart categorization and SKU optimization enhance efficiency.

2. Micro-Fulfillment Centers (Dark Stores)

- Strategically located in high-density areas for rapid dispatch.
- Compact, tech-driven warehouses reduce delivery times.
- Robotics and automation for order picking and packaging.

3. Advanced Order Processing Systems

- AI-driven order batching groups multiple deliveries efficiently.
- Automated workflows minimize processing delays.
- Integration with cloud-based platforms for real-time tracking.

4. Last-Mile Delivery Optimization

- Smart route planning reduces travel time and fuel costs.
- Dynamic traffic updates ensure riders take the fastest path.
- Rider allocation algorithms match orders with nearby couriers.

5. Mobile-First Customer Experience

- AI-powered search and personalized recommendations.
- One-click ordering and seamless payment options.
- Real-time order tracking with push notifications.

6. Cloud Computing & Data Analytics

- Scalable cloud infrastructure supports high order volumes.
- Data analytics optimizes pricing, promotions, and stock levels.
- AI-driven insights enhance customer engagement and retention.

7. IoT & Smart Warehousing

- IoT sensors track temperature-sensitive items (e.g., groceries).
- RFID technology automates stock monitoring.
- Warehouse robots enhance picking accuracy and speed.

8. Payment & Security Infrastructure

- Encrypted transactions ensure customer data protection.
- AI-powered fraud detection minimizes risks.
- Multiple payment gateways including UPI, wallets, and BNPL.

9. Sustainability & Green Tech

- Use of electric vehicles (EVs) for last-mile delivery.
- AI-driven eco-friendly packaging solutions.
- Carbon footprint tracking and reduction strategies.

The seamless integration of AI, automation, cloud computing, and IoT enables Q-Commerce to deliver orders within minutes.

Dark Stores & Micro-Fulfillment Centers: The Hidden Engine

In the fast-paced world of Quick Commerce (Q-Commerce), speed is everything. The secret to delivering orders within minutes lies in Dark Stores and Micro-Fulfillment Centers (MFCs)—the hidden engine powering rapid deliveries.

1. What Are Dark Stores?

Dark stores are small, strategically located warehouses designed solely for fulfilling online orders. Unlike traditional retail stores, they don't serve walk-in customers but act as distribution hubs for ultra-fast deliveries.

Key Features of Dark Stores:

- **Hyperlocal Placement** – Located close to high-demand urban areas.
- **Limited but High-Demand Inventory** – Stocks essential, fast-moving items.
- **Tech-Enabled Operations** – AI-driven stock management and automation.
- **Optimized Layout** – Designed for rapid picking and packing.

2. Micro-Fulfillment Centers (MFCs): The Tech-Driven Evolution

Micro-Fulfillment Centers (MFCs) are compact warehouses equipped with robotic automation and AI to process orders faster. They are often embedded inside existing retail stores or standalone hubs.

How MFCs Work:

- **AI-Powered Inventory Management** – Ensures high availability of top-selling products.
- **Automated Picking & Packing** – Uses robotics to speed up order fulfillment.
- **Seamless Integration** – Connected with Q-Commerce platforms for real-time order tracking.

Example: A grocery chain might install an MFC within its store, allowing customers to get their orders in under 15 minutes without affecting walk-in shoppers.

3. The Role of Dark Stores & MFCs in Q-Commerce

Factor	Dark Stores	Micro-Fulfillment Centers
Purpose	Fulfillment hubs for online orders	Small-scale fulfillment within/near retail stores
Location	Standalone, urban areas	Inside stores or close to customers
Tech Usage	AI for inventory, manual picking	AI, robotics, and automation
Speed	10-30 minutes delivery	5-15 minutes delivery

Both models reduce last-mile delivery time, cut costs, and boost efficiency, making them the backbone of Q-Commerce success.

Optimizing Last-Mile Delivery for Instant Gratification

In **Quick Commerce (Q-Commerce)**, last-mile delivery is the most critical and expensive part of the supply chain. It determines whether customers get their orders within minutes or experience frustrating delays. To meet the instant gratification demand, Q-Commerce companies optimize last-mile delivery through technology, efficiency, and smart logistics strategies.

1. Hyperlocal Fulfillment for Speed

- Dark Stores & Micro-Fulfillment Centers (MFCs) are placed strategically in high-demand areas to reduce delivery distances.
- AI-powered inventory ensures that the right products are always available.
- Impact: Orders are dispatched in under 2-3 minutes, reducing overall delivery time to 10-30 minutes.

2. Smart Route Optimization & Dynamic Dispatching

- **AI-based delivery algorithms** assign the nearest rider for the fastest route.
- **Real-time traffic analysis** ensures couriers avoid congestion.
- **Order Batching** – Multiple orders from the same zone are grouped for efficiency.
- **Impact:** Faster ETAs, fuel cost savings, and lower carbon emissions.

3. Gig Workforce & On-Demand Delivery Models

- **Hybrid Fleets** – A mix of full-time, gig workers, and third-party logistics (3PL) for flexible delivery.
- **Predictive Demand Forecasting** – AI adjusts rider availability based on peak hours.
- **Crowdsourced Delivery Apps** – Riders are dynamically assigned based on proximity.
- **Impact:** Ensures 24/7 availability and reduces idle time for couriers.

4. Micro-Mobility & Sustainable Delivery

- **E-bikes, scooters, and drones** improve speed in dense urban areas.
- **Eco-friendly initiatives** reduce delivery carbon footprints.
- **AI-optimized delivery routes** minimize energy consumption.
- **Impact:** Faster delivery in traffic-heavy zones and lower operational costs.

5. Real-Time Tracking & Customer Experience

- **Live Order Tracking** – Customers can monitor their deliveries in real-time.
- **Instant Notifications** – Alerts on rider location, estimated time of arrival (ETA), and delays.
- **Chat Support & AI Assistance** – Helps with order updates and complaints.
- **Impact:** Higher customer satisfaction, reduced anxiety, and better trust in the platform.

6. Automated Lockers & Contactless Deliveries

- **Smart Lockers** – Customers can pick up orders from secure, automated drop points.

- **Contactless Drop-offs** – Riders leave deliveries at doorsteps for convenience.
- **QR Code or OTP-based Verification** for secure pickup.
- **Impact:** Enhances delivery flexibility and reduces failed delivery rates.

7. AI-Powered Fraud Detection & Security

- **Geofencing** prevents fake location updates from riders.
- **Proof of Delivery (POD)** via photo verification and customer confirmation.
- **AI-driven fraud alerts** detect suspicious orders or misuse of promo codes.
- **Impact:** Ensures trust, reliability, and safety in the Q-Commerce ecosystem.

Final Thoughts

By leveraging AI, automation, and innovative logistics, Q-Commerce platforms ensure deliveries are ultra-fast, reliable, and efficient. Companies like Zepto, Getir, and Gopuff are redefining last-mile delivery for instant gratification, making speed **their** biggest competitive advantage.

Inventory & Demand Forecasting: Getting It Right Every Time

In **Quick Commerce (Q-Commerce)**, where deliveries happen in minutes, having the right inventory at the right place is critical. Unlike traditional retail, Q-Commerce deals with high-demand, fast-moving products that need constant replenishment. This is where AI-driven demand forecasting and inventory optimization come into play.

1. AI-Powered Demand Forecasting

- **Predictive Analytics** – AI analyzes historical sales data, customer behavior, and market trends to forecast demand.
- **Real-Time Adjustments** – Dynamic stock replenishment based on live orders and seasonality.
- **Hyperlocal Demand Analysis** – Identifies product preferences in different locations.
- **Impact:** Reduces overstocking and prevents stockouts, ensuring that the most in-demand items are always available.

2. Smart Inventory Management for Dark Stores & MFCs

- **Decentralized Stocking** – Inventory is distributed across **micro-fulfillment centers (MFCs)** for faster access.
- **AI-Optimized Stock Allocation** – Ensures best-selling products are stored in **high-demand zones**.
- **Just-in-Time (JIT) Restocking** – Minimizes excess storage and optimizes shelf life for perishable goods.
- **Impact:** Ensures **faster fulfillment**, reduces **wastage**, and **cuts storage costs**.

3. SKU Prioritization & Product Mix Optimization

- **High-Demand Product Selection** – AI filters products based on **historical sales trends, local preferences, and seasonality**.
- **Dynamic SKU Rotation** – Products are rotated based on changing consumer demand patterns.
- **AI-Driven Product Substitutions** – When an item is out of stock, AI suggests **alternate products** that match customer needs.

- **Impact:** Higher order fulfillment rate and seamless shopping experience.

4. Data-Driven Replenishment & Supplier Integration

- **Automated Stock Replenishment** – Inventory gets auto-ordered when it reaches a low threshold.
- **Direct Supplier Integration** – AI forecasts real-time restocking needs and places orders automatically with vendors.
- **Fast-Track Procurement** – Partnerships with local suppliers for just-in-time inventory management.
- **Impact:** Ensures products are always available without overstocking, reducing waste and costs.

5. Handling Seasonal & Surge Demand

- **Weather-Based Forecasting** – Predicts sales spikes (e.g., hot beverages in winter, cold drinks in summer).
- **Event-Based Planning** – Prepares inventory for special events like festivals, sports matches, and public holidays.
- **AI-Driven Promotions** – Adjusts stock based on ongoing discounts and marketing campaigns.
- **Impact:** Ensures inventory meets demand peaks, **preventing** lost sales during high-traffic periods.

6. Real-Time Inventory Tracking & Visibility

- **Cloud-Based Inventory Management** – Live inventory status accessible across all fulfillment centers.
- **Low-Stock Alerts** – AI sends real-time notifications for restocking.
- **Shrinkage & Loss Prevention** – Monitors theft, damages, and expired stock with automated tracking.

- **Impact:** Reduces errors, prevents stockouts, and keeps operations efficient and cost-effective.

Final Thoughts

Getting inventory & demand forecasting right is the key to Q-Commerce success. Companies like Zepto, Blinkit, and Gorillas use AI-driven stock management to ensure that every product is available exactly when customers need it.

Growth & Market Expansion

Scaling a Quick Commerce Startup

Scaling a Quick Commerce (Q-Commerce) startup requires a strategic approach to optimize operations, expand reach, and enhance customer experience. Here are the key areas to focus on:

1. Infrastructure & Technology Scaling

- **Robust Tech Stack:** Ensure your app and backend systems can handle increased order volume without lag or downtime.
- **AI & Automation:** Leverage AI for demand forecasting, automated order processing, and delivery route optimization.
- **Cloud Infrastructure:** Use scalable cloud solutions to support real-time inventory tracking and seamless transactions.

2. Expanding Dark Stores & Fulfillment Centers

- **Micro-Fulfillment Centers (MFCs):** Set up dark stores in high-demand areas to speed up order fulfillment.

- **Inventory Optimization:** Use predictive analytics to stock the right products in the right locations.
- **Strategic Partnerships:** Collaborate with wholesalers and suppliers for efficient stock replenishment.

3. Last-Mile Delivery Optimization

- **Fleet Expansion:** Scale your own delivery fleet or partner with third-party logistics providers.
- **Rider Efficiency:** Optimize routes using AI and GPS tracking to reduce delivery time.
- **Hybrid Delivery Models:** Use a mix of hyperlocal delivery, bike couriers, and autonomous delivery solutions (like drones or robots).

4. Customer Acquisition & Retention

- **Loyalty Programs:** Implement reward systems to encourage repeat purchases.
- **Personalized Marketing:** Use AI-driven recommendations based on purchase history and browsing behavior.
- **Referral & Subscription Models:** Offer incentives for customer referrals and subscription-based ordering.

5. Geographic Expansion

- **Market Research:** Identify high-potential cities or regions with strong demand for Q-commerce.
- **Localized Approach:** Tailor offerings based on local preferences and shopping habits.
- **Regulatory Compliance:** Ensure adherence to local business laws, delivery regulations, and data privacy policies.

6. Financial Planning & Unit Economics

- **Cost Efficiency:** Optimize procurement, warehousing, and logistics to reduce operational costs.
- **Revenue Streams:** Explore additional monetization options like in-app advertising, premium delivery services, and brand partnerships.
- **Investment & Funding:** Secure funding from venture capitalists or strategic investors to fuel growth.

Hyper local Strategies: Winning in Every Neighborhood

Scaling a Quick Commerce (Q-Commerce) startup isn't just about speed—it's about precision. Hyperlocal strategies help businesses cater to the specific needs of each neighborhood, ensuring faster deliveries, better product selection, and stronger customer loyalty. Here's how to win in every neighborhood:

1. Micro-Market Selection: Knowing Where to Expand

- **Data-Driven Expansion:** Use AI-driven insights to identify high-demand areas based on order frequency, population density, and spending habits.
- **Localized Store Placement:** Set up dark stores or micro-fulfillment centers (MFCs) within a 2-3 km radius of high-order zones to minimize delivery time.
- **Community-Centric Offerings:** Study neighborhood demographics and tailor product assortments accordingly (e.g., organic products in affluent areas, budget-friendly essentials in middle-class neighborhoods).

2. Neighborhood-Specific Inventory & Pricing

- **Smart Stocking:** Use predictive analytics to keep inventory aligned with hyperlocal demand patterns, reducing waste and stockouts.

- **Dynamic Pricing:** Implement real-time pricing adjustments based on demand trends and competitive analysis within a specific locality.
- **Local Brand Collaborations:** Partner with local vendors and small businesses to offer exclusive, locally preferred products.

3. Optimized Last-Mile Delivery for Hyperlocal Speed

- **Decentralized Rider Hubs:** Place delivery personnel strategically across neighborhoods for faster order pickups and drop-offs.
- **AI-Powered Routing:** Use geospatial analytics to optimize routes and minimize delays during peak hours.
- **Eco-Friendly Deliveries:** Introduce electric bikes, cycle couriers, or drone deliveries for sustainability in dense urban areas.

4. Hyper-Personalized Marketing & Engagement

- **Neighborhood-Specific Campaigns:** Leverage geotargeted ads and push notifications to promote offers based on local events or buying trends.
- **Community Engagement:** Sponsor local events, collaborate with neighborhood influencers, and offer location-based discounts.
- **Loyalty & Referral Programs:** Reward repeat customers with exclusive discounts or perks for referring neighbors.

5. Leveraging Local Partnerships for Market Penetration

- **Tie-ups with Local Businesses:** Collaborate with neighborhood kirana stores, bakeries, and fresh produce vendors to expand inventory without high warehousing costs.

- **Hyperlocal Influencers:** Engage local social media personalities to drive trust and awareness in specific neighborhoods.
- **Delivery Aggregators & Gig Workers:** Partner with local delivery networks during peak times to scale flexibly.

6. Real-Time Customer Insights & Adaptation

- **Live Feedback Loops:** Gather instant feedback from customers via app interactions and surveys to improve service.
- **Rapid Iteration:** Adjust product catalogs, delivery strategies, and marketing approaches based on local customer behavior.
- **Customer Support Localization:** Provide multilingual customer support and localized chatbot interactions to improve user experience.

Winning at the Hyperlocal Level

Success in Q-Commerce depends on deep neighborhood-level insights, localized offerings, and real-time adaptability. By blending technology with community engagement, startups can build a hyperlocal ecosystem that ensures not just fast deliveries—but a lasting presence in every neighborhood.

Marketing & Customer Retention in the Age of Instant Delivery

In the fast-paced world of Quick Commerce (Q-Commerce), acquiring customers is just one part of the game—retaining them is what drives long-term profitability. With consumers expecting near-instant deliveries, personalized experiences, and competitive pricing, businesses must craft innovative marketing and retention strategies.

1. Hyper-Personalized Marketing: The Key to Customer Stickiness

Consumers in the Q-Commerce space expect speed, convenience, and relevance. Personalization is the bridge between a one-time buyer and a loyal customer.

AI-Driven Personalization

- **Behavior-Based Product Recommendations:** Leverage AI to suggest frequently bought items or complementary products based on past purchases.
- **Dynamic Push Notifications:** Send hyper-personalized offers based on order frequency, preferred shopping times, and browsing history.
- **Geo-Targeted Offers:** Use real-time location data to promote local store discounts, neighborhood-specific bundles, and time-sensitive deals.

Loyalty & Rewards Programs

- **Gamified Loyalty Systems:** Offer points for every order, which can be redeemed for discounts, exclusive products, or free delivery.
- **Subscription-Based Models:** Introduce membership perks like priority deliveries, exclusive deals, or cashback on frequent purchases.
- **Referral Incentives:** Encourage customers to invite friends with discounts for both the referrer and the new user.

2. Speed-Optimized Customer Engagement Strategies

Engagement must be real-time, responsive, and convenient—mirroring the instant nature of Q-Commerce.

Real-Time Customer Support

- **Chatbots & AI Assistants:** Implement instant AI-powered chat support to resolve common queries within seconds.
- **24/7 Human Support:** Combine automation with human touch for complex issues, ensuring a seamless customer experience.
- **Proactive Issue Resolution:** Offer compensation (discounts or credits) for late deliveries, missing items, or poor service experiences.

Social Media & Community Engagement

- **User-Generated Content (UGC):** Encourage customers to share their unboxing experiences, quick meal preps, or instant needs met by your service.
- **Micro-Influencer Marketing:** Partner with local influencers for authentic brand promotion and neighborhood-level engagement.
- **Live Shopping & Flash Sales:** Host time-sensitive Instagram or TikTok live shopping events with exclusive deals for immediate conversions.

3. Leveraging Data for Retention & Re-Engagement

Understanding customer behavior through data helps predict churn and re-engage users effectively.

AI-Powered Churn Prediction

- **Early Warning Systems:** Identify customers who haven't ordered recently and send personalized win-back offers.
- **Abandoned Cart Recovery:** Use SMS, email, or app notifications to remind users about items left in their cart.
- **Feedback Loops:** Conduct micro-surveys post-purchase to identify pain points and optimize future experiences.

Exclusive & Limited-Time Offers

- **Flash Sales:** Create urgency-driven campaigns with limited-time discounts.
- **Personalized Discounts:** Offer individual discounts based on past purchases or seasonal buying patterns.
- **Bundle Deals & Cross-Selling:** Promote curated product combos that cater to specific needs (e.g., "Midnight Snacking Pack" or "Morning Essentials Kit").

4. Retention-Focused Logistics & Service Excellence

Fast delivery isn't enough—it must be consistently reliable, seamless, and delightful.

Predictive Delivery Accuracy

- **Live Order Tracking:** Keep customers engaged with real-time delivery updates and estimated arrival times.
- **AI-Optimized Fulfillment:** Reduce order errors and ensure products are stocked in the right locations for ultra-fast fulfillment.
- **Preferred Delivery Slots:** Give customers flexibility to choose precise delivery time windows.

Surprise & Delight Strategy

- **Random Freebies:** Occasionally add small complimentary items (chocolates, trial products) to surprise loyal customers.
- **Thank You Notes & Personalization:** A simple "Thank You, [Name]" on the packaging or inside the app fosters emotional connection.
- **Instant Customer Recovery:** If an order is delayed or incorrect, offer instant app credits or discounts on the next order.

Winning in the Instant-Delivery Era

To dominate Q-Commerce, businesses must acquire, engage, and retain customers at lightning speed. The combination of hyper-personalization, real-time engagement, predictive analytics, and flawless fulfillment is the formula for long-term success.

Challenges & Future of Quick Commerce

Profitability vs. Speed: Can Quick Commerce Sustain Itself?

Quick Commerce (Q-Commerce) thrives on ultra-fast deliveries, instant gratification, and seamless customer experience—but can it remain financially sustainable in the long run? The fundamental challenge lies in balancing speed with profitability. Here's a deep dive into whether Q-Commerce can sustain itself and what strategies can ensure long-term viability.

1. The Profitability Challenge in Q-Commerce

Q-Commerce operates on thin margins, high operational costs, and an intense demand for speed. Key cost drivers include:

- **Last-Mile Delivery Costs:** Delivering small orders in under 30 minutes increases per-order logistics expenses.
- **Dark Store & Micro-Fulfillment Costs:** Setting up and operating hyperlocal warehouses adds fixed overhead.
- **High Customer Acquisition Costs (CAC):** Heavy marketing spend is required to attract and retain customers.
- **Low Basket Size:** Average order values (AOVs) tend to be small, making unit economics tricky.

Without careful optimization, these challenges can erode profitability, leading to unsustainable business models.

2. Can Speed & Profitability Coexist?

Yes—but it requires strategic adjustments in several areas:

Optimizing Delivery Economics

Speed is essential, but delivery costs must be controlled. Strategies include:

- **Batching Orders:** Grouping multiple orders from nearby locations to reduce per-order delivery costs.
- **AI-Powered Route Optimization:** Ensuring efficient rider allocation and shortest delivery paths.
- **Hybrid Delivery Models:** Combining gig workers, full-time riders, and third-party logistics partners for flexibility.

Increasing Order Value & Frequency

Profitability improves when customers order more per transaction or order more frequently.

- **Minimum Order Value for Free Delivery:** Encourages customers to add more items to meet a threshold.
- **Bundling & Subscription Models:** Offering curated product packs and membership programs for recurring revenue.
- **Personalized Upselling & Cross-Selling:** AI-driven recommendations to increase basket size.

Dark Store Efficiency & Inventory Management

- **Demand Forecasting:** Using AI to predict stock needs and prevent overstocking or stockouts.

- **Supplier Negotiations & Private Labels:** Partnering with vendors for better pricing or launching in-house brands.
- **Zonal Pricing & Dynamic Inventory:** Adjusting product availability and pricing based on hyperlocal demand.

Sustainable Customer Acquisition & Retention

- **Referral & Loyalty Programs:** Reducing CAC by turning existing users into brand advocates.
- **Hyperlocal Marketing:** Targeted ads and community engagement for lower-cost conversions.
- **Superior Customer Experience:** Faster refunds, better packaging, and personalization to build brand loyalty.

3. The Future: Can Q-Commerce Be Profitable?

Q-Commerce can sustain itself if companies shift from burning cash for growth to smart optimizations for profitability. The path forward involves:

- **Strategic Expansion:** Prioritizing high-density urban areas where operational costs per delivery are lower.
- **Automated & AI-Driven Operations:** Reducing inefficiencies in warehousing, delivery, and marketing.
- **Diverse Revenue Streams:** Leveraging in-app advertising, premium memberships, and brand partnerships.
- **Balancing Speed & Costs:** Ensuring ultra-fast delivery doesn't come at the expense of bottom-line losses.

Verdict: Q-Commerce is at a crossroads. Companies that find the right balance between speed, efficiency, and profitability will dominate the space—while those stuck in a discount-driven, high-burn model may struggle.

The Role of AI & Automation in Quick Commerce

Quick Commerce (Q-Commerce) thrives on speed, precision, and efficiency, making AI & automation essential for scalability and profitability. From inventory management to last-mile delivery, AI-driven solutions are revolutionizing the way Q-Commerce operates. Let's break down the key areas where AI and automation play a game-changing role.

1. AI-Driven Demand Forecasting & Inventory Management

One of the biggest challenges in Q-Commerce is stocking the right products at the right locations to minimize delays and prevent stockouts.

How AI Helps:

- **Predictive Demand Forecasting:** AI analyzes historical sales data, weather conditions, local events, and customer behavior to forecast demand with high accuracy.
- **Smart Inventory Replenishment:** Automated restocking ensures dark stores and micro-fulfillment centers never run out of high-demand products.
- **Dynamic Product Placement:** AI optimizes warehouse layouts by placing fast-moving products closer to pick-up areas, reducing order processing time.
- **Impact:** Up to 40% reduction in stockouts and 30% improvement in inventory turnover rates.

2. AI-Powered Order Fulfillment & Warehouse Automation

Fulfilling orders within minutes requires speed and accuracy— something AI and automation can enhance significantly.

How AI Helps:

- **Robotic Process Automation (RPA):** Automated picking and packing systems speed up order processing.
- **Smart Picking Algorithms:** AI prioritizes and sequences picking tasks for efficiency, reducing fulfillment time.
- **Automated Quality Checks:** AI-powered vision systems inspect product quality before dispatch.
- **Impact:** Increases order processing speed by 50% and minimizes human errors in fulfillment.

3. Last-Mile Delivery Optimization with AI

Delivery is the most cost-intensive part of Q-Commerce, but AI-driven logistics can make it more efficient and cost-effective.

How AI Helps:

- **Route Optimization:** AI calculates real-time traffic, weather, and road conditions to suggest the fastest delivery routes.
- **Dynamic Fleet Allocation:** AI assigns orders to delivery riders based on location, availability, and past performance.
- **Delivery Time Predictions:** Machine learning models provide accurate ETAs, improving customer satisfaction.
- **Drone & Autonomous Deliveries:** AI powers self-driving delivery bots and drone deliveries in select areas.
- **Impact:** Reduces delivery time by 20-30% **and** lowers fuel costs by 15-25%.

4. AI-Enhanced Customer Experience & Retention

Fast delivery is not enough—personalization and engagement are key to retaining Q-Commerce customers.

How AI Helps:

- **Personalized Recommendations:** AI suggests products based on past purchases, browsing habits, and local trends.
- **Chatbots & Virtual Assistants:** AI-powered chatbots handle customer inquiries, refunds, and complaints 24/7.
- **AI-Driven Loyalty Programs:** Predicts which customers are at risk of churning and offers targeted discounts or rewards.
- **Impact:** Boosts repeat purchases by 25-40% **and** reduces customer churn by 30%.

5. AI-Powered Pricing & Promotions

Competitive pricing is crucial in Q-Commerce, and AI ensures pricing is always optimized for profitability.

How AI Helps:

- **Dynamic Pricing Models:** AI adjusts product prices in real-time based on demand, competitor pricing, and inventory levels.
- **Smart Discounting:** AI analyzes customer buying behavior to offer personalized discounts without hurting margins.
- **A/B Testing for Promotions:** AI continuously tests different promotions and marketing campaigns to find the most effective ones.
- **Impact:** Increases profit margins by 10-15% while keeping customers engaged.

6. Fraud Prevention & Risk Management

With instant transactions and cash-on-delivery options, fraud prevention is critical for Q-Commerce success.

How AI Helps:

- **Fraud Detection Algorithms:** AI flags suspicious transactions, preventing payment fraud.
- **Address Verification & Geo-Fencing:** Ensures delivery addresses are legitimate, reducing failed deliveries.
- **AI-Powered Rider Monitoring:** Detects anomalies in rider behavior, preventing theft and inefficiencies.
- **Impact:** Lowers fraud-related losses by up to 50%.

The Future of AI & Automation in Q-Commerce

AI is no longer just an enhancement—it's a necessity for Q-Commerce to scale profitably. As machine learning models become more advanced, we can expect:

- Fully **autonomous warehouses** with robotic sorting and packing.
- **AI-driven hyperlocal marketing** that predicts customer needs before they arise.
- Widespread **drone and self-driving deliveries** for ultra-fast fulfillment.

Final Verdict:

AI & automation are the backbone of sustainable Q-Commerce reducing costs, improving speed, and enhancing customer experience. The startups that invest in AI-first operations today will dominate the Q-Commerce market tomorrow.

Sustainability & Ethical Challenges in Rapid Delivery

Quick Commerce (Q-Commerce) has revolutionized shopping by providing instant deliveries within minutes. However, the speed and convenience come with significant sustainability and ethical challenges, from environmental concerns to labor exploitation.

Let's explore the hidden costs of rapid delivery and how businesses can address them responsibly.

1. Environmental Impact: The Cost of Speed

Carbon Footprint of Instant Deliveries

- **Increased Traffic & Emissions:** Frequent, small deliveries lead to more vehicles on the road, increasing CO_2 emissions.
- **Inefficient Last-Mile Logistics:** The need for speed often results in single-package deliveries, increasing fuel consumption.
- **Short-Lived Packaging Waste:** Single-use plastic bags, excessive packaging, and disposable containers contribute to environmental pollution.

Sustainable Solutions:

- **Green Delivery Fleets:** Use electric bikes, e-scooters, and eco-friendly vehicles to cut emissions.
- **Batching & Route Optimization:** AI-powered logistics to group multiple orders together, reducing unnecessary trips.
- **Sustainable Packaging:** Shift to biodegradable materials, reusable packaging, and minimal waste solutions.
- **Impact:** A switch to EVs and optimized routing can reduce Q-Commerce delivery emissions by up to 40%.

2. Labor Exploitation & Rider Welfare

The Human Cost of 10-Minute Deliveries

- **Intense Work Pressure:** Riders often have unrealistic delivery targets, leading to burnout and unsafe driving.

- **Low Wages & Unfair Contracts:** Many gig workers are underpaid, lack social security benefits, and have no job stability.
- **Health & Safety Risks:** Speed-focused policies increase road accidents, putting riders' lives at risk.

Ethical Solutions:

- **Fair Pay & Benefits:** Introduce minimum wage guarantees, performance bonuses, and healthcare coverage for riders.
- **Safe Delivery Timelines:** Shift from ultra-fast (10-15 min) to a more sustainable 30-45 min model to reduce pressure.
- **Accident Insurance & Safety Training:** Offer protective gear, driving safety workshops, and mandatory insurance coverage.
- **Impact:** Companies investing in rider well-being see higher retention rates and better customer satisfaction.

3. Excess Consumerism & Waste

Encouraging Overconsumption

- **Impulse Buying Culture:** Q-Commerce promotes unnecessary shopping, increasing food waste and product discards.
- **Excess Returns & Reverse Logistics:** Free returns encourage unsustainable shopping habits, leading to more emissions.

Sustainable Commerce Practices:

- **Eco-Friendly Product Selection:** Promote local, organic, and ethical brands in Q-Commerce catalogs.
- **Smart Inventory Management:** AI-driven demand forecasting to reduce waste in dark stores.

- **Responsible Consumer Nudging:** Incentivize bulk orders and subscription models to cut down frequent, small purchases.

Impact: AI-driven inventory optimization can cut food waste in Q-Commerce by up to 30%.

4. Ethical Sourcing & Supply Chain Transparency

Unchecked Supplier Practices

- **Many Q-Commerce startups** prioritize speed over ethical sourcing, often overlooking worker exploitation in supply chains.
- **Local retailers & farmers struggle** to compete with corporate-backed dark stores, affecting neighborhood economies.

Ethical Supply Chain Solutions:

- **Fair Trade & Local Partnerships:** Support local farmers, small vendors, and ethical suppliers.
- **Transparent Sourcing Labels:** Clearly mark sustainable and ethically sourced products in the app.
- **AI-Powered Monitoring:** Use blockchain and AI to track fair labor practices in supplier networks.

Impact: Fair-trade integration improves brand reputation and customer trust, boosting long-term retention.

5. The Dark Store Dilemma: Local vs. Corporate Control

The Risk of Monopolization

- **Dark stores** are displacing neighborhood retailers, shifting power to large corporations.

- **Over time**, small businesses face declining foot traffic as customers opt for app-based ordering.

Solutions for Local Business Inclusion:

- **Hybrid Models:** Allow local kirana stores and supermarkets to operate as micro-fulfillment hubs.
- **Vendor Integration:** Enable small businesses to list products on Q-Commerce platforms.
- **Regulations for Fair Competition:** Governments may need to set policies preventing monopolistic practices.

Impact: Inclusive models preserve local economies while still enabling rapid delivery services.

The Future: Can Q-Commerce Be Ethical & Sustainable?

- Yes—but only if companies shift from "ultra-fast" to "smart-fast."
- Sustainability, fair labor practices, and responsible consumerism must be at the core of Q-Commerce models.
- Tech-driven solutions (AI, EVs, blockchain) will be key to balancing speed with ethics.

Final Verdict:

The 10-minute delivery race is unsustainable without ethical and environmental reform. The Q-Commerce leaders of tomorrow will be those who prioritize both speed and sustainability.

The Future of Quick Commerce: Trends & Predictions

Quick Commerce (Q-Commerce) is evolving rapidly, driven by technological advancements, shifting consumer expectations, and sustainability concerns. As the market matures, companies will need to innovate beyond speed to remain competitive. Here are the top trends and predictions shaping the future of Q-Commerce.

1. Shift from "Ultra-Fast" to "Smart-Fast" Deliveries

The 10-minute delivery model has proven operationally expensive and environmentally unsustainable. Instead, the future will favor a "Smart-Fast" approach:

Prediction:

- **Deliveries** will gradually shift to a 30–60 minute model to balance speed with profitability.
- **Companies** will batch multiple orders together, reducing logistics costs and carbon footprint.
- **Consumers** will accept slightly longer delivery times in exchange for lower fees and eco-friendly options.

Impact: Lower operational costs, improved sustainability, and higher margins.

2. AI-Driven Hyperlocal Expansion

Hyperlocal fulfillment is the backbone of Q-Commerce. AI-powered demand forecasting will refine inventory management, ensuring the right products are available in the right neighborhoods.

Prediction:

- **AI-powered dark stores** will adjust inventory dynamically based on real-time consumer behavior.
- **Localized product assortments** will dominate—offering region-specific items based on customer preferences.
- **Autonomous fulfillment centers** will increase, using robotics for ultra-fast picking and packing.

Impact: Reduced inventory wastage, better product availability, and improved efficiency.

3. The Rise of Subscription & Membership Models

With high customer acquisition costs (CAC), Q-Commerce players will shift toward retention-focused models like subscriptions and loyalty programs.

Prediction:

- **Amazon Prime-like memberships** offering free deliveries, cashback, and exclusive discounts will become common.
- **AI-driven loyalty programs** will reward repeat customers with personalized incentives.
- **Pre-scheduled deliveries** for essentials (groceries, pet food, baby products) will increase via subscription services.

Impact: Higher customer retention, predictable revenue, and lower CAC.

4. Autonomous & Sustainable Last-Mile Delivery

The last-mile is the most costly and resource-intensive part of Q-Commerce. Automation and green logistics will be critical.

Prediction:

- **AI-powered delivery routing** will minimize travel time and fuel consumption.
- **Electric Vehicles (EVs) & drones** will increasingly replace gas-powered delivery fleets.
- **Autonomous micro-warehouses on wheels** (mobile dark stores) will move inventory closer to demand hubs.

Impact: Lower costs, reduced carbon emissions, and greater scalability.

5. Growth of Quick Commerce in Tier 2 & 3 Cities

So far, Q-Commerce has thrived in major urban centers, but the next wave of expansion will focus on smaller cities with growing digital adoption.

Prediction:

- Companies will optimize unit economics to make rapid delivery viable in Tier 2 & Tier 3 markets.
- Partnerships with local businesses and kirana stores will replace the need for expensive dark store networks.
- Vernacular language app experiences and regionalized marketing will drive adoption in non-metro markets.

Impact: Expansion beyond metro cities, increased market penetration, and new customer acquisition.

6. AI-Enhanced Customer Experience & Personalization

Customers will expect not just speed, but personalization—and AI will play a key role in delivering hyper-personalized experiences.

Prediction:

- **AI-powered recommendation engines** will suggest frequently purchased items for faster checkout.
- **Real-time delivery tracking with predictive ETAs** will become more accurate and interactive.
- **Voice & chat-based ordering** via AI assistants (Alexa, Google Assistant, WhatsApp) will rise.

Impact: Higher order frequency, better customer retention, and seamless shopping experiences.

7. Sustainable Q-Commerce: A Key Differentiator

Consumers are becoming more environmentally conscious, forcing Q-Commerce startups to integrate sustainable business models.

Prediction:

- **Eco-friendly packaging** will become standard, with bans on plastic bags and non-recyclable materials.
- **Green delivery choices** (EV delivery, carbon-neutral options) will be provided at checkout.
- **Local sourcing & ethical supply chains** will drive a shift towards sustainability-focused commerce.

Impact: Brand differentiation, regulatory compliance, and improved customer trust.

8. Super-App Ecosystem & Embedded Q-Commerce

Standalone Q-Commerce apps will integrate into broader digital ecosystems, offering more than just groceries or essentials.

Prediction:

- **Q-Commerce** will merge with FinTech & Social Commerce, allowing in-app payments and group buying.
- **Super-app models** (like WeChat, Meesho, or JioMart) will integrate instant delivery within ride-hailing, food delivery, and e-commerce platforms.
- **Retailers & grocery chains** will build their own Q-Commerce channels, reducing dependence on aggregators.

Impact: Higher user retention, diversified revenue streams, and greater customer convenience.

The Road Ahead for Quick Commerce

Q-Commerce is no longer just about speed—the future belongs to AI-driven efficiency, sustainability, and customer-centric innovation.

- **Ultra-fast** will evolve into Smart-Fast.
- **AI & automation** will drive hyperlocal efficiency.
- **Sustainability** & ethical commerce will define market leaders.
- **Embedded** commerce & super-apps will fuel deeper integrations.

Final Verdict:

The Q-Commerce market is expected to grow at a CAGR of 25-30% over the next five years. Startups that balance speed with profitability and sustainability will dominate the next phase of Quick Commerce.

Disclaimer

The information provided in this book is for educational and informational purposes only. While every effort has been made to ensure the accuracy and relevance of the content, the author and publisher make no guarantees regarding its applicability to individual circumstances.

The strategies, insights, and case studies presented are based on industry trends and personal expertise. However, business success depends on various external factors such as market dynamics, competition, regulations, and operational execution. Readers are encouraged to conduct independent research and seek professional advice before making business or financial decisions.

The author and publisher disclaim any liability for any loss, damage, or inconvenience caused as a result of reliance on the information contained in this book. Any references to companies, products, or services are for illustrative purposes only and do not constitute endorsements.

By reading this book, you acknowledge that you are solely responsible for any actions taken based on the content and agree to hold the author and publisher harmless from any consequences.

www.ingramcontent.com/pod-product-compliance
Lightning Source LLC
LaVergne TN
LVHW010041070326
832903LV00071B/4718